New Jobs Full Of Wonder
20 jobs kids and adults must hear about now

By Al Phasso

Illustrations by Mary Hasanpour

Dedication:

To my son and to all members of Generation Alpha, who will shape the world of the future.

Introduction to Parents:

Dear grandparents, parents, and caregivers,
In today's interconnected world, one of the greatest gifts we can offer our children is to prepare them to face the new global labor market. But what does that mean? How can we lead and support our young learners? Well, we must encourage our children to be curious and to think on a global scale. The more we do so, the more they will discover their place in their world.
If you too are worried about being left behind in this era of information and ultra-fast stimulation, then here are twenty new jobs which you can familiarize yourself with. We should talk to our children more about these things. These jobs will be in high demand when our 'little ones' are of working age.

Happy Reading!

Introduction to children:

Sooner than you know, you will be an adult with a real job. Perhaps you will be a salesperson, an architect, a vet, a dentist, a blogger...

A Meteo Rainmaker

Like Louis, you could launch amazing micro-rockets into the clouds which cause rain to fall back on the Earth. This will make the farmers very happy because rain is needed for the crops to do well so that there can be a large harvest.

Would you also want to make it rain?

How about **a Driverless Car Traffic Controller**?
Elliot can decide where all the cars, taxis and trucks move
to make sure there are no accidents.

Do you think it would be cool to control the cars on the
roads?

Or maybe you could be **an Urban Farmer specialized in aquaponics**?
Maya and Eden grow fruit and vegetables using large fish tanks. The water has nutrients for the plants and the fish feed on the roots of the plants.

Would you enjoy growing plants and raising fish to sell?

Why not be **a Chef cooking insects**?
Charlotte cooks delicious scorpion burgers. She also prepares tasty cricket soups.

Could you imagine even crazier recipes?!

Or would you rather be a Firefighter Drone Pilot? Rauny pilots magnificent firefighting-drones and saves human and animal lives.

And you, would you have the skills
to do this job?

You are lucky to have so many
jobs to choose from ...

Maybe you should be **a Deepwater Data Diver**?

Jack dives into the ocean to repair large boxes filled with information called data. He uses special tools to make sure that people receive internet service at the speed of a rocket.

Would you like to have marvelous underwater adventures?

Or do you want to be **a Digital Privacy Detective**?
Mata searches and deletes personal information that people don't want to have on the Internet. She helps people become invisible on the Web.

Would you love to protect other people's secrets?

Or do you wish to catch bad guys as **a Cyber Cop**?
Paul fights against the attacks of the "pirates on the internet". He protects other people's computers by blocking viruses and stopping scamming attacks.

Would you like to protect the internet for everyone on the planet?

How about **a Crowdfunding Specialist**?
Angel helps others to make their
dreams come true.

He collects money from Internet users around the world. This is possible thanks to his creativity and his great communication skills.

Would you love to help people to share their great ideas with the rest of the world?

If you love drawing and making things then you could choose to become...

An Upcycling Designer

Lola transforms waste materials into new products. As if by magic, she changes toothbrushes and other used plastic objects into jewelry and she turns cardboard boxes into furniture.

And you, could you imagine other surprising things?

Or you could be **a 3D Designer**…
Donna draws and creates awesome objects straight out of her imagination. Thanks to her computer and a fantastic printer, she can produce everything in three dimensions (3D). This means that she can make toys, vases, shoes, whatever she wants with her incredible printer.

Would you like to use your creativity to produce new things?

Or maybe be **a Big Data Scientist**?

"Big Data" these are all the numbers, words, photos and videos, called "data" which circulate the world. The amount of data on the Web is enormous and keeps growing non-stop. Steven knows how to understand all this data and can solve problems even before they appear.
Abracadabra! He can tell you where to place a wind turbine so it catches the most wind.

Would you enjoy giving meaning to data just as Steven does?

You could become a good **Robotics Engineer** like Leo…
Robots are made to do things that are too boring or too dangerous for humans. Leo, the master of the robots, knows how to write instructions in robot language. In this way, he can tell the robots to efficiently do the work that humans want them to do.

Would you enjoy being such a great guide?

Or why not become **a Guardian of Space Safety**?
Neil removes the remnants of old rockets and old satellites sent by humans into space. Then he places them in a space dump to avoid any accidents.

Do you look forward to making outer space less dangerous?

How about **a Virtual Presentation Coach**?
Anna teaches others how to bring out the best of themselves when presenting. She advises them how to smile at the camera and speak clearly.

And you, would you like to help others give the best version of themselves?

Or do you wish to be **a Re-Wilder**?
Tom is an agricultural scientist who "repairs" the damage done to the Earth by people, factories, and cars.

Would you also cherish taking care of the Earth?

Or like Nina be **a Nano-Scientist**?
Nina takes tiny pieces of matter, breaks them up and puts them back together in amazing ways. These smart materials, such as super strong and foldable plastics, can even be used to make cars.

Would you be interested in creating new materials?

Or do you wish to be **a Tele-Surgeon**?
Charlie carefully uses an incredible robot scalpel, which can be used to operate on human beings or animals from very far away.

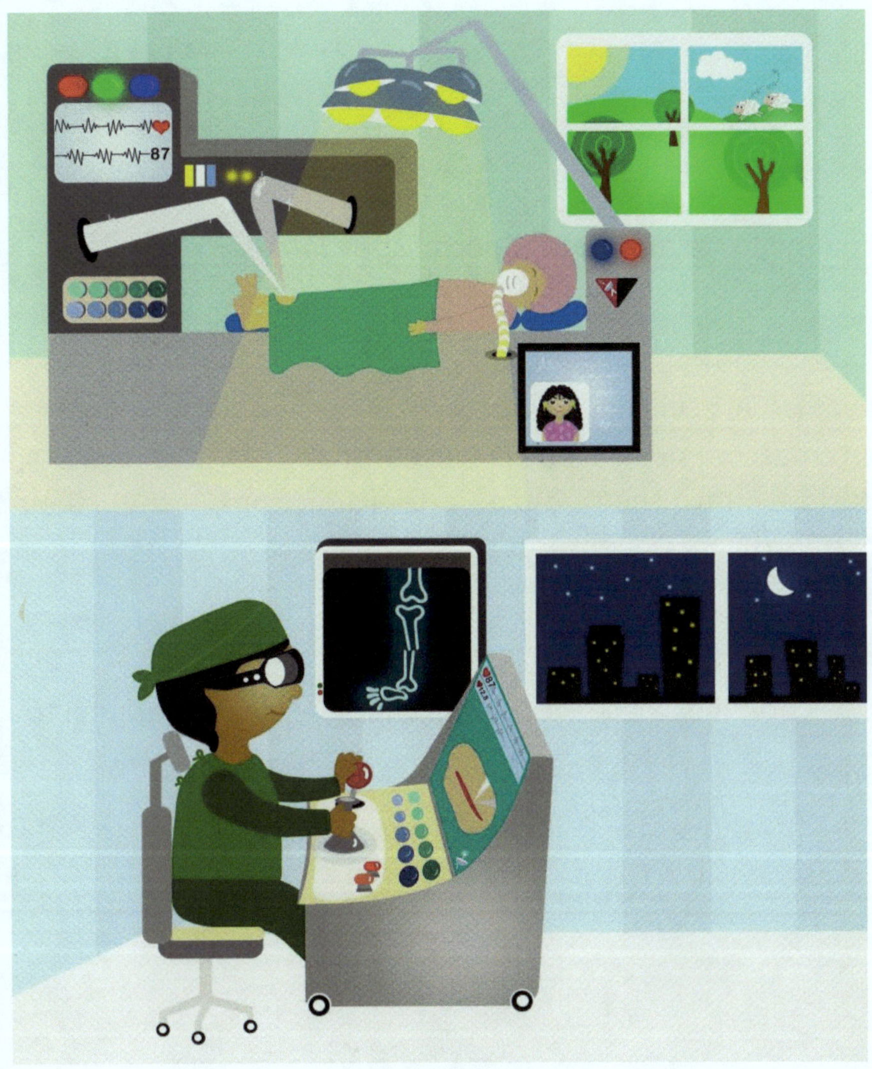

Would you be happy to offer medical care from the other end of the world?

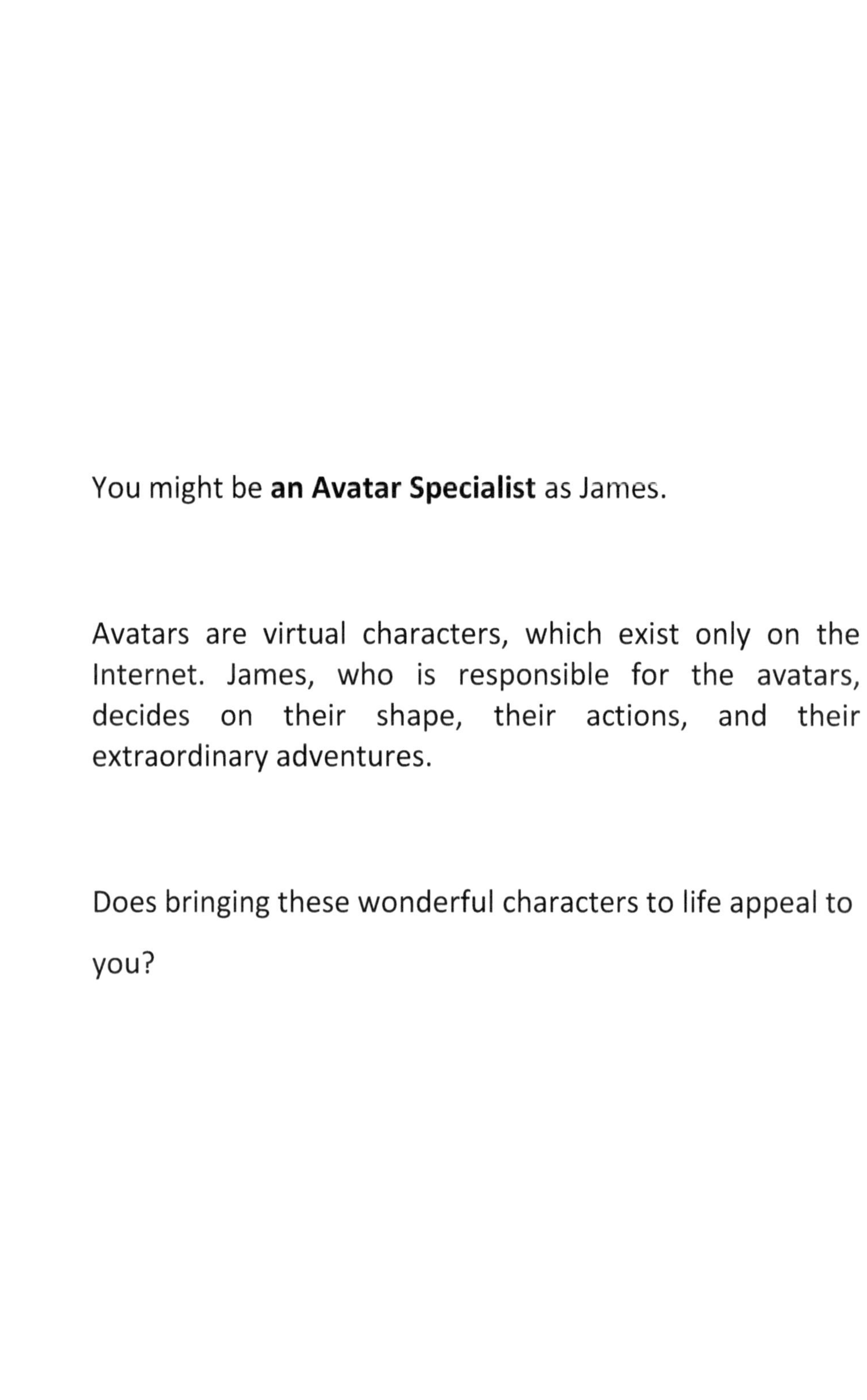

You might be **an Avatar Specialist** as James.

Avatars are virtual characters, which exist only on the Internet. James, who is responsible for the avatars, decides on their shape, their actions, and their extraordinary adventures.

Does bringing these wonderful characters to life appeal to you?

3D

Maybe you should be **a Researcher in bio-inspiration**?
Mary makes use of great ideas taken from nature to help
her solve problems. For example, she might experiment
with snail slime to make a new, odorless kind of glue.

And you, would you have the patience to observe animals
and plants?

To children:

You have so many possibilities! These jobs are just some examples of jobs from the future. So keep your eyes wide open, take the time to look carefully around you to discover the best of the world. Then, you will surely find what it is you really want to be.

To adults:

To know more about these jobs and to be able to answer your children's questions, visit the website **alphasso.com**. These jobs have not been invented. Adults can find more information at Dr Frey's website :
-**Dr Thomas Frey**, futuristspeaker.

Thank you for reading this book.

Appreciations:
Thanks to Mary who is a fantastic illustrator!
Thanks to Doud for his patience, his critical eye, and his optimism. Thanks to my family for their support and ideas, and to the Jindal family for their technical contribution towards the completion of this book.
And finally thanks a million to the Loudon family for helping to make this book a more pleasurable experience.

About the Author and Illustrator:

The Author:

(Photo Credit: Azusa Uchida)

I am a French middle-aged mom of a very energetic little Elf. He loves to listen to stories so he can begin to understand the world that surrounds him...and I love to investigate so I can picture his future. It seems to go well beyond what we all know! Please visit us at **alphasso.com**

The Illustrator:

I'm a Persian illustrator with childlike spirit who lives in Vienna. I try to put pieces of my soul in each illustration to stimulate the child's imagination and provide for little adventure seekers a better understanding of the world. If children ask a lot of questions or smile while looking at my illustrations then they are surely enjoying them.

Copyright Page